The Ohio State University Press/*The Journal* Award in Poetry

for my mother and father

Antidote

Corey Van Landingham

The Ohio State University Press | Columbus

Library of Congress Cataloging-in-Publication Data
Van Landingham, Corey, 1986–
Antidote / Corey Van Landingham.
p. cm. — (Ohio State University Press/The journal award in poetry)
Summary: In Corey Van Landingham's Antidote, love equates with disease, valediction is a contact sport, the moon is a lunatic, and someone is always watching. Here the uncanny co-exists with the personal, so that each poem undergoes making and unmaking, is birthed and bound in an acute strangeness. Wild and surreal, driven by loss, Antidote invites both the beautiful and the brutal into its arms, allowing for shocking declarations about love: that it is like hibernation, a car crash, or a parasite. It soon becomes clear that there is no antidote for grief or heartbreak, that love can, at times, feel like violence, and that one may never get better at saying goodbye.

ISBN-13: 978-0-8142-5187-4 (pbk. : alk. paper)
ISBN-10: 0-8142-5187-0 (pbk. : alk. paper)
ISBN-13: 978-0-8142-9343-0 (cd-rom)
ISBN-10: 0-8142-9343-3 (cd-rom)
1. Poetry, Modern—21st century. I. Title. II. Series: Ohio State University Press/The journal award in poetry.
PS3622.A585494A83 2013
811'.6—dc23
2013009412

Cover design by Thao Thai
Type set in Janson
Printed by BookMobile

The paper used in this publication meets the minimum requirements of the American National Standard for Information Sciences—Permanence of Paper for Printed Library Materials. ANSI Z39.48–1992.

9 8 7

Contents

Acknowledgments

Much gratitude to the editors of the journals in which the following poems first appeared, sometimes in slightly different forms:

AGNI: "The Making of a Prophet"
Barn Owl Review: "Other Techniques for Elegant Boatmanship"
Best New Poets 2012: "Tabernacle for an Adolescence" (reprint)
Blackbird: "[engagement]," "To Have & To Hold," "To Have & To Hold," and "To Have & To Hold"
The Collagist: "Diurnal," "Parallax Disguised as Endless Disappointment"
Colorado Review: "This World is Only Going to Break Your Heart"
Copper Nickel: "Against the Reification of Isadora Duncan"
Crazyhorse: "Orchard" and "What You Will Encounter"
cream city review: "Confessional" and "The Chair & the Birdcage"
Devil's Lake: "The Architecture of Fathers"
Hayden's Ferry Review: "Valediction Lessons"
Indiana Review: "Eclogue," "When You Look Away, the World," and "While Terrified of Branches, Making Fun of Moon"
The Journal: "Antidote"
Kenyon Review: "Elegy in Which I Refuse to Turn Away"
Linebreak: "Elegy" and "Valediction Lessons"
Mid-American Review: "Last Year at Marienbad"
Redivider: "Spill"
The Southern Review: "During the Autopsy"
Tampa Review: "Autonomy, Landscape, Terrible Love"
Third Coast: "Tabernacle for an Adolescence" and "What You Erase Knits Back Together"
Typo: "Decreation"
Washington Square Review: "And Badly, Too" and "Bestiary"
West Branch: "The Louse"
"Autonomy, Landscape, Terrible Love" was chosen by the Association of Writers and Writing Programs for the 2012 Intro Journals Project Award.
"This World is Only Going to Break Your Heart" and "Valediction Lessons" were featured by *Verse Daily*.
"When You Look Away, The World" received the 2011 *Indiana Review* ½ K Prize, judged by Ander Monson.

With the deepest gratitude for all of my teachers along the way, especially Donald Platt for his endless generosity and wisdom, Mary Szybist, Jerry Harp, Marianne Boruch, Dan Morris, and Mary Leader. Thank you to Brittany Cavallaro, Sara Eliza Johnson, Josh Diamond, Jessica Farquhar, Jacob Sunderlin, Rosi Moffett, Greg Allendorf, Jessica Jacobs, Lindsey Alexander, Mario Chard, Josh Wild, Allison Hutchcraft, Josh Kaminski, and Kenny Tanemura for keen eyes and big hearts. I would like to thank everyone else at Purdue University and *Sycamore Review* for their support and friendship. Gratitude to the Bread Loaf Writers' Conference and to all the fine writers and friends met on the mountain. My greatest appreciation for the love of Joyce Snyder, Rainy Olsen, Drew Olsen, Aaron Hersh, Hannah Barton, Adam Lefton, and Patrick Brennan. To everyone at Ohio State University Press and *The Journal:* thank you for making this book possible. To Kathy Fagan: thank you for the best phone call of my life. But most importantly I want to thank my father, who I know would have been proud, and my mother, for absolutely everything. This book is for you.

There is scarce any thing that hath not killed somebody; a hair, a feather hath done it; nay, that which is our best antidote against it hath done it; the best cordial hath been deadly poison.

—John Donne, VII. Meditation

Autonomy, Landscape, Terrible Love

Never mind cycles.

Never mind the way parasites train for survival or how bears turn their bodies off continually inside some hollowed out tree trunk where love is nothing, yet is still something that sleeps.

Bridges have changed my favorite river into a prize. Here is the covered bridge you walk through when you're feeling old-timey. The way you think crossing over a body

of water equals acquiring the other side.

There, you tell me half-truths, like the wind
must be inchoate somewhere.

Because this is mostly about who
buries whom, we have no sense of the pressure that might have created us,
or where our bodies went to.

Where our bodies went to, so quickly away.
It is hard to get the compass to spin because it is dividing here

from not here.

I wait to exit through the forest of substitutes.
Everything (branches) are standing in for something else (units
of measure). There is how far I am from you

and how far the ground is from injury.

The bleached pines will survive us if I don't open my eyes.
All those maps for hatching under bark, for breathing
into fresh-dug holes—

they can't locate me.

Nor the river when I imagine the bridge collapsed.

The trees allow their diseases to burn out in daylight so that I won't see how they glow when they suffer.

One might lie down, undisturbed, beneath a tree and wake up to the moon fusing itself to one's tongue as if it might repair what little longing is left waiting there. What little longing awaits,

spinning under glass.

Tabernacle for an Adolescence

The science experiments gone awry. The skulls of vermin
and the black silk ribbon strung through them. The lamp
she tied them to. The light she never left on. The place
to bury cicada husks. The place to buy purple face glitter.
The surface disorder. The forest and that one clearing
swollen and yellow through the hacksaw trees. The sexy
forest where she chose one man over another with her
mouth. The fizz in the medicine. The stomach of noise.
The faucets rusted out on the side of the house like sentinels.
The floodlights turned off. The lake with all those leeches.
The way they mirrored fucking—find something and attach
yourself. The dock built in the middle of the lake she could never
bring herself to swim to. The fish that appeared to be drowning.
The uncanny light on the teeth they never had. The water plants
recoiled so as not to have to touch her skin. The scream
in the middle of the night in the town she forgot owned her.
The hoot of the train as it mocked her staying there. The apples
she whittled into pipes and the weed she forgot in another state.
The lunch she forgot at her desk and the mold on the wheat
bread. The man on the trolley who told her he'd certainly
save her if she was drowning. The microscope her mother
practiced scrutiny on. The antidote to all those pills she was
taking. The walls with scrawled song lyrics and the irony in the
rap music she memorized. The foreign exchange student and
all her cigarettes. The stuffed owl in her grandmother's house.
The little boxes she collected. The boxes made in woodshop to
hide her pills. The forest her father drove into to take her home.
The dress he made her out of an old tweed jacket to hide her
bare body. The instruments her mother used to pick her apart.
The camera her father set up in the living room to reconstruct
her face. The birthday cake slapped on her lap and the sleeves
of the dress dragging in the chocolate frosting. The candles fallen
to the carpet around her socks and the fire she might have been
able to stomp out, had she not been still in the forest, a stump
of a girl. The fire that started every time she came home and all
those photographs nuzzled into her hand when she woke up
in the trees. The mouths of fish hung above her. Proof
she was not some experiment. The proof that she was.

Valediction Lessons

Bromeliads hold their water close for later.
And have I ever been held close for later?
Here is the fossa where you store, what, a
tangle of sounds? And see the insects throwing
their bodies against our bodies? Hear the wind-
pipe's rattle, sea grass, and a humming wound?
The star-pit is a far-flung lamentation reflected
back by the sea. The sand dollar is an extremely
flattened, burrowing sea urchin. Though I am
a bonfire I am not so bent on visiting the
Laconicum. The sun through the leaves prints
patterns of skeletons on the soil. I never said
I wanted to be retooled and left trusting in a cold
desert. And there are still knees to kiss, a logician's
broken music to dreamproof. A celebration of
the impossibility of eyelashes, of having an exit
from the flesh? Here is an extremely flattened place
for people to go who cannot clean the salt stains
from their feet. And tears are not liquefied brain
but maybe they could preserve a creature or
be made into a nice necklace. The pinecone feels
inevitable in the hand, but who has breath left
to spend on little things like walking away.

Elegy in Which I Refuse to Turn Away

Hospice recommended we starve him. I did.

I can sleep all day. Things happen & my father dies.

I go to Italy. I fall apart under Tintoretto, those

smudgy crucifixions. In another life, I am promised

to a lawyer. I have a wedding chest heavy with linens.

When I wake in a small boat filling with ocean,

my father sews the white dress into my skin. I am

given medicine to help me sleep. People are hired

to stand around my bed, & hold my wrists down while

I writhe. This isn't what I imagined, but isn't necessarily

worse. The wedding plate shatters, my once beloved

reads me my Miranda rights. Owls keep crashing

into the bedroom window, mid-day, & I'm not

allowed to touch them, am made to kneel at a safe

distance. My father always makes me turn away

while he snaps the owl's neck. He is saving it.

I know this. From something worse. But I have

the right to see what happens to their yellow eyes.

Do they stay open. Does he stroke their wings to

calm them down until, in his hands, they go slack.

Anything I say can and will be used against me

in the middle of the night. Boat I dream fills with

talons. I have the right to use them how I want.

The Chair & The Birdcage

No one has come to see them, and no one will. *We belong together*
their morning refrain. In the early light the Chair and Birdcage debate

the pastoral. Its over-arching despair. All those damn bleating sheep.
The exogenous shepherd and his devilish superstitions. The split-open

head of the cow. Irreverent, elegant flying formations of some dark,
too-large birds. Here the Cage weeps, not for the Chair whose leg is now

perpetually half-breaking, but for itself. For what it has lost. The Chair
insists the shepherd is wise and noble. Because it would like to be

knocked around, a little more touching. The Chair insists the sheep *want*
the cane, the shears. And they are facing each other, the Chair,

the Birdcage, they can see that this means everything. And they are trying
to reason, they are the last two left. They will start a new life together.

It will be sweet, it will exist under a constant, dizzy, sugar-spell of rain.
There will be baths with dried flowers poured into the water. There will be

swooning and warm milk and a small porch to watch the weather.
Chair says: *Turn around.* Chair says: *Turn around and shut up.* Cage obeys—

this must be what love is like. The Birdcage swivels its hips to the field
below and sees all the animals it never got to hold. How absolute it seems,

the distance. *Tie up your hair.* The horses that must have once been wild.
Close your eyes. The lightning-blackened branches. The stranger it will never

touch. *Close your eyes.* The long unbraiding of the far-below river the river
the river and the shepherd with his face hidden as he bends to drink.

Antidote

Given against devotion. Given against proclamations
of love at Dover and the sting of the tide pool

anemone. Given against enemies, digital
sex, fog banks, proclamations of love over

the phone. Given against fake sugar. Given
against distinctions of house and home.

Given against your inclination to gather
all my hair into your fist and pull hard.

Given against your sweat-stained pillow,
the mice in the walls. Given against

proclamations of love over whiskey
that was just another hiding place.

Given against this gulf weather that
keeps killing all my mint. Given against

brevity, the inclination to run, your
ability to pin me there and there and

there, proclaiming your love, all your
unbearable love, all that love you feel

when you're cleaning your gun right
in front of me to counteract some

proclamation of *I'm leaving you* or
I left you a long time ago or *Don't.*

Don't kill the dog just because I loved
him. Don't chop down the fig tree because

I loved the seeds between my teeth. Don't say
I didn't warn you that I had never found

an antidote against the inclination to fall asleep
while you recited your favorite songs into

my mouth, given against your mouth, given
against owning something so dismissive as

a body given against another body given
up to another to be touched and retouched.

Spill

Dear boat-sink
Dear bathtub
I am with you here

                        & here

Bird slick   mud mask   half-life

Barataria Bay needs a box
for its belongings

Have you practiced your definition
for relief

Do tug boats still cannon

    for bodies

Dear body count
Dear bother
I have a mouth

                  for you to fill with mud

I have a mouth for ibis   for sand crab   for sea turtle

all the pretty things
I put in my mouth
to forget

           I have a mouth

The Louse

> *Most lice are specialists, feeding on a single species to whose fur or feathers their claws are adapted.*

You'll find a louse opening itself to the procedure
of flight, which must be sublime in its wingless

mechanics, its feather-lock, upsweep unhooked
from the earth. Yes, Sappho, things have

turned out badly for us. I name every injury
like it was a comet. There are ghosts that swim

through me and I cannot drown them. So
still we are left here, parsing beauty. The thin,

rib-like structures of the louse. The piece of stone
imprinted with its lost armor. When we split

from ape, the louse followed, loyal to its host,
duly splitting itself—*I simply want to be dead*—

in two to follow new form, new being.
And the creature with its specialized claws held fast

to the bird as if they were made for each other,
as if what does not let go in the air is something

worth keeping. These small monsters. They will not
save you, Sappho. They will not undo the *koma*

beauty threw you; the trance beauty threw you into.

Decreation

because I am forgotten by the blue bottle
and hive   by the acacia's mouth and the mirror's
fogged mouth   because inside the pocket
of recovery there is a green deep-oceaned fish
whose erasure theories spin through
the downed ship   pagan ship of being built
the wrong side upward   fish behave as bullets
in the offhanded emergency that night takes into
its palm   because this is a canyon experience
little quarrels held up to the chorus
I mean light   a procedure for being sutured
and pinned to a sky of glass   because
a gun is a piece of silver foil hologramming
inside a fisheye   when eaten the ocean
drains back into the mineral garden
I am left standing here   composed
of silicates and black milk and black-eyed susans
I'm doing it again   expand delay expand   delay
I came here tonight to say it's hard not to take
Gauguin personally   I mean steer away
from mercy   the white-fleshed fruit
my fish   I came here tonight because
it's hard not to take   tonight I came here

What You Will Encounter

Something is always spilling—
bird shape, bird shape—
from the sky we created.

Weeds tendril the fence
you painted blue.

The boat's still out.
Your father or my father
is captain or anchor

or the largemouth bass
tugging the line.

When the owl took
the marking post, where we buried
what was left of the dog—

a head of fur—
the lake couldn't have slapped

time back any farther.
This is an emptied way
to talk about convergence

and vanishing points.
Geese. The skyline breaks,

breaks. There are no newly-
dead. You would have
liked it, how the moon

organzas the water.
But you were late.

For all this I didn't have.
Or you didn't show up.
I tried on all the bodies

hanging around the cabin
until I found a note

in your mouth—
it's good, like this.
I wore your skin suit

until I fell asleep.
Then I got less beautiful.

Less patient.

The Architecture of Fathers

I.

They move like haunted houses, which means
they don't move, but are moved inside. Each
bump, every cough in their crawlspace is enough
to collapse the roof. The roof hasn't been around
for years, not since their growth in the attic pushed
it off. And at night they let the owls swoop in.
Nurses. The hospital bed lowered so that their chest
mirrors the sky—blackest tumor in every X-ray.
The walls of their ribs reveal branches covered
in snow. Mice crawl inside them, make the owls go
lustful. But only they hear all this. Feel it, too.
The wind coursing in rivulets down their arms,
how it stings open the windows. When insects
tire of light, they cover the faces of the fathers.

II.

When children fill a haunted house, it looks
more silly than scary. The hills you see outside
and the tapering clouds about to erupt with hail,
the loneliness of being emptied, trees like drifters.
Are you ever afraid the old leaves will stay inside
you forever. Or that all this will leave, no more
mice to find stiff on the kitchen floor. The storm
that will be the attic's last upheaval, filling it
with an ice that melts down to the pit of your
back, plants a stone, which will not grow.

What Will Be Untold

The stranger you were seeing came from river country.
He was practicing talk. You told him you came to
this country small and naked and he understood like

a good dog. This was before the chicken livers
and the spattering oil, the small quick burns.
Burns your mouth couldn't keep from lying about,

so when you spoke to the stranger, every word was
a burial. The graveyard you were hiding in your
chest opened up for him and he was amused. It was

all wrong. His arm kept draping over your shoulder
and all the words to your favorite songs were
clenched in the teeth of the garbage disposal. Still,

airplanes landed. Mothers called. The stranger sat up
in your bed, heavy with his new language. It was all
O Death and Baby Baby Baby. He leaned over

to whisper it to you like you were an entire, muted
audience. He was asking questions like What Kind
Of Beasts Are We and What Name Do You Want

In My Acknowledgments Page. Something felt stolen.
You couldn't even clap. You couldn't ask for an encore,
and couldn't decide if it felt like freedom or a murder.

This World Is Only Going to Break Your Heart

Space has been shut off for summer, etc.
In the last shuttle launched,
I am told to love a piece of earth. Then metal.
Then the optics behind the things I hold
in my hand.

I am told: be simple. Only love
what you can bear to break in half.
Paintings I once owned adhere to the ceiling,
so that I walk under ponds with lily pads like drowned hats.

I don't often feel like walking,
having heard the announcement that I am stuck out here
with Decisions To Make. What graffiti will be
unbirthed. Which hills will turn white with bones. Pathogens.

When I flinch
into an unimpressive sleep, I will dislodge some unimpressive planet
with a terrain that shakes under a red sky like a syphilitic man.
I try not to sleep. There is day,

then there is later day.
Sure, there are things that I miss. Tornadoes.
The idea of brothers. Distinguished dogs with cauldrons of summer saliva.

Once, I even felt holy.
It was at the throes of an orange tree.
I could have been stoned to death and still would have sung out
Tongue! Barren tongue!

There are ghosts up here. But they were shut off
long ago, when I tried to put my arms around them and was told
I'd have to choose between the slaughterhouse and the morgue.

I retaliated with apathy.
I cut off my ears.

During the Autopsy

"She hid it well," they say, gathered around the body. Some standing
in the gallery think of their god, big as an ox, and are thankful

for once not to be the chosen one. Her stomach opened to reveal
the tree growing inside her, seeming to take root near the navel,

branching out between the ribs. Thick bark falling away under
the scalpel. A man worries a pair of bats from her throat. Wings

raw from rubbing against the wood, panicky. Flesh houses
milk-white bulbs, new life, pale like her throat, a nice one.

A throat to be stroked nightly by some woodsman. And the bats
are the most vibrant black the man has ever seen. Their wings

seem to be living separately from their bodies, trying to detach.
And so he pictures the woman in the same light, tree its own

creature, not hers, not *her*, as he takes a bone saw to a branch,
or, with the smaller ones, snaps them off with his hands.

One must, at times, learn to ignore the body. In a dream
the man was once patron saint of ships. Not only did he build

the most sea-worthy ships of his small town, but he blessed
all the vessels in the shipyard. Walking from wood hull to wood

hull, he would press his hands against them, speak to them with his
palms. And they would speak back. The man would carry their

stories with him from sleep, so that, in the morning, his hands were
still full with them, seemed to anchor him to the mattress, hands

heavy with whale bones and kelp nests. With crates of rotting
fruit, the smell of too many men together, skin sloughing off

like flakes of *sel de mer*. And the man had forgotten all this, until
his hands were around the trunk, growing like his own thigh,

and he could see each layer of the cut-into wood, which looked
not unlike each layer of the thick skin of the belly, the woman

not a woman, but a tree now. The tree, with his hands around it,
sang into him a high-pitched song, song of a siren, a woman's

voice asking to be returned to the sea. Any sea. And as he
washed his hands after, thorough as always, as he walked

home in the rain to his wife. As he drank the glass of water
she had poured him from a clay pitcher, he could feel that voice

in his throat, and that night he woke—suddenly, salt water
covering his entire body—to that other woman's song.

To Have & To Hold

I go to a forest where they give away animals that help you sleep. Bones tunnel into the ground where they reappear later like old roots.

*

Easy.

*

No one keeps me at arm's distance and whispers too much fur into my mouth. No one staying in the ground can remember the sound of you brushing your teeth. No one making animal sounds underneath a nightmare.

*

It turns me on, this morning with all the birds fallen out of the trees. I discard all my old déjà vus.

*

If I am never on a horse without you, you never existed, right?

*

I hate the light that forces the day like a fox breaking into an egg.

*

I rearrange the only shadow left to me. The trees. The animals are encrypted with all my old recipes for winter soups, so light passes through them.

*

You would have told me that's impossible. That everything has to have its own shadow.

*

It is incredibly important, what I do not say to the fox I am handed. Anything can hunt the hand that feeds it.

*

But it is winter. I am cold all the way through. There is nothing inhuman enough to eat with a spoon.

The Making of a Prophet

for Adrienne Rich

Keep it small   they said   Keep it small
or the city will form a mouth   Be careful
not to say mouth   or world   Don't say
body   Drink your coffee   Fuck it
There are gum wrappers on the sidewalk
that reflect all those predator drones
You can almost see them see you   You
flip your hair   You preen   You touch
yourself but you can never see them   They
can always see you   There is a room
full of men making anything possible   It is
the loneliest thing   making up worlds
Watching others live their little lives   Keep
it small   the men are telling you   Wave to
the sky   No   to a bird you are no longer
allowed to name   and may no longer exist
You've been selected for a very particular
Task   All you have to do is talk and talk
and talk and not say anything at all   This
should be easy   They say that   too

[engagement:]

engagement: A pledge, a pawn, encumbrance. The parties that were bound. Covenant. The shadow on top of the shadow of doubt. The shadow of a chicken hawk circling the pasture. We call it redwing to forget talons. We call it engagement, as in, appointment. A festivity. A brief period of occupation. We call it this to forget ourselves, which are on top of our other selves, which can never be joined with another, as a shadow will never merge directly with the body. As in, someone already in line for the dance. Damsel with her book of those in waiting. *We regret to inform you that C was unable to meet her engagements.* Promise of a life with willow branches above the door, and the man left behind. We regret to inform you of the hawk, the fox, the newly-freezing night. We regret to inform you of the unknowable predator, the gravel found lodged in the throat, the year of feathers. An obligation, or bias. The fact of being entangled. The fur found caught in barbed wire, what a fence can't keep out, and all the animals it tries to hold on to forever. The circle of feathers around the coop. The fact of being entangled, of never being good with hands, or knots. Of never being able to cut along a straight line, of being too inclined to scissors, to the hard beak, the glinting tooth. Dog digging up the potatoes, the miscarriage, the ring of hair. The fact of understanding the predator more than the prey. A battle, a conflict, the act of crossing swords.

Elegy on Sea Legs

I go to islands I've never heard of and name
        every rock. Each stillness is the sister I never had.

I should be back in Oregon burning my father.
        I am back in Oregon with an empty book

of matches, two hands. The valley where I learned
        pronunciation does not recognize my fingers

against it. They have become common, as happens
        to those who require love. Meat sheds its divinity

in my mouth, becomes another word for animal.
        In the future, I will treat each stem like it is good.

People die when I'm not looking. When surrounded
        by water, there are less ways to be outsmarted,

touched. I've heard the island of Madeira burned
        for seven years. Epitaphs survive on dry land.

There are certain barenesses that replace you.
        That's what I carved into an oak tree once.

When you name something wild Laura, she
        tilts her head in a man-made way. Every dog,

every doll, has made adjustments. There are
        the frocks that hide our bodies. A fine wood

ash covers each fruit I hunt. One cliff
        overlooks the ocean, so every cliff overlooks

the ocean, so is my new reduction theory.
        The lunatic moon never had a father, so.

While Terrified of Branches, Making Fun of Moon

Various methods for torture must have been divined here. Why else
would the branches look like that.
Like they deserved a body,
for being so sickly. Like somewhere, there is a hotel room
full of them—branches—and they can't even smell the fire
blistering on next door.
They can sleep like that.

—

The moon is adequate. The stars,
adequate. When the oak rots out, a little motor starts,
spiraling down into a basement of wires
unconnected and glorious.
Someone will sing about this on the radio,
and she doesn't even know me.

—

The birds wide-awake and anxious.
No one wants coins on their eyes, to receive
my greeting card, the collective consciousness
I've copyrighted: the moon is still out,
wearing the wrong hat, the wrong nose.

Orchard

No, you can't get the best apples from the market.
Not those bitter Kazakh strains, the swallow-me-whole ones,
or the unfortunate looking fruit. They must be rooted for like a hog,
face-down in the orchard, breathing up soil. This is what plants do.
Easy enough. Not that you have to understand them.
Besides, when the sky hurtled the fruit down no one hushed
or wept. But that's the wrong myth, the one with wings.
The right apples will take you into terror
for a moment and hold you close as a Tilt-a-Whirl
holds your organs up in the air before placing them back,
carefully, into their correct locations. It is desirable
to be puzzlesque, to think about the body in pieces.
Are you brave inside you? You must be, out here in the orchard,
spine to the night, sensing someone standing behind you.
Hear her big gloves as she claps, the slow clap,
as she moves her mouth in concentric circles. You'd forgotten
howling, or what you thought it might sound like.
Her hands start to pluck you; you're a tooth pulled
from the earth, and it is not good and you scream until she stuffs
an apple in your mouth, pushes the tongue back,
not choking your speech, but drawing it down
into her well. The best apples have been tossed there.
You have to bob for them. Quiet. You have to use your teeth.
The best apples are burnout stars getting time off
for bad behavior. They can't ever go back, you know this.
You can't crawl back out of the well. This isn't a myth.
No, you're not crying, you're just playing the part of the ghost.
The audience is sweating you out mid-coitus. Can you hear it?
You're being pushed through the smallest space in the universe,
smaller than a seed, and, I don't have to say it,
you already know, but you won't come out whole.

Valediction Lessons

Though it looks like it should be named *plague*,
        a gathering of starlings making the sky grow dark

is a *murmuration.* I once thought the word *singed*
        was really *sung*, and now there are no new animals

left to be grouped and named something romantic.
        I once thought language a gift. I am learning different

techniques for survival, what to call each black wing.
        In a documentary, lions gather around some carcass,

looking hungrier as they feast. The sun momentarily
        blinds the camera, so that when I can see again

the legs have already been devoured. Yet the spines
        underneath acacia leaves prick predators' tongues.

The small ridges on kudus' horns are formed to lock
        together during mating season's battles. Tonight, love,

I am crying out your name into another man's mouth.

Parallax Disguised as Endless Disappointment

Some days I am living in a country that kisses women
before it kills them. Some days it builds them a home

of cloth bandages and tells them to stand on their heads.
The ones who fall fall out of the wound that is

home, which is the one dank place they can never
get back to. Some days the sun looks so huge

I duck for cover. I buy large, black tarps to drape
over my head. I reflect every stranger's face.

What they want. My forehead shines *Sandwich,*
shines *Free gas for a year. A little violence to remind*

how real this all isn't? Some days I am living with
a weather that never liked its own name. It acts out

against my tree house windows. I fall into a rain
barrel which is really just old weather and

isn't too keen on its backwater origins either.
Some days men look at me, and some times

they don't. Other times all the little girls
on the pedestrian bridge are carrying wands like

machetes and are the color of old bathwater.
The ocean is under disguise as acid-washed jeans.

The fish are rusty safety pins holding up the sagging
waist. When they try to touch each other, they open

yet another wound. Infection. Seaweed is a dirty
bandage, thus the house one can't return to.

Pin-pricks, the kiss I never wanted. I am the strange loop
siphoning the saltwater through a crazy straw.

Watering the garden so that nothing will grow back.
Only the tamped-down spoons. The spoons taken to

the persimmon taken to my mouth. Some days
all the old spoons taste faintly of silver.

I tell myself *everything in this wish-cloud is mine.*
Some days that helps like *hair of the dog*, myth

to make one more miserable. Some days the women
cut my hair so short it feels like it might bleed.

This is an airspace for all the monologues
worth flying away from. Some days coffee seems

ridiculous and some days it feels like apotheosis.

All the Sworn on, Sworn off Truths

I came to you as an experiment. The hypothesis was
not good. I was Petri dish and you peeked around

a curtain—bashful scientist—before unlocking
the house. You never should have unlocked the house.

Under your heat, I grew a blanket of mold that kept
us sick for an entire winter. Mucus and sweaty hands

fooled our better selves. You had a better self.
In bed, you told me if you had the vial in your hand

to destroy each human, you would. For all intents
and purposes, this was foreplay. But I outgrew the

plastic container, pitched around the kitchen while
you were working. You were always working. Away

at the lab you made astonishing things. I was always
leaving pieces of myself in the cabinet, behind

the cardamom pods, the chicken stock. In one wild
search to make myself whole before your return,

I found a ring planted inside a bed of agar. I had
forgotten honor. It was all so man-made. Diamond,

red jelly, the see-through house of disease. I wanted
to fossilize right there on the linoleum. To become

a lighthouse on some shore I had never seen. If
erected just right, I could have remembered what

was expected of all this. The old men behind the
two-way mirror in the bedroom. That they watched

us grow sicker and sicker. That this was all my fault.

Romance Novel after the Car Crash

Hazard lights piling up—how the imagination
makes a night sky of them, an uncanny aurora
borealis of bystanders, the extra cars, extra bodies,
the *Oh*, the *Oh, no*. Then. The stones gathered

in the dark, filling the pockets of the nightgown,
the bringing them back to bed, like a lover might,
like there's some error in how to be drowned,
but no, no confusion here, just weights to hold

a body down, stones that feign a boozy touch
unreturned—that spite, the *No sex tonight* trick—
and it's shocking, really, how many people
will gather around a body, but not touch it.

How it takes the one blonde twenty-something
rushing from the ambulance to lift a wrist onto
her lap, press her fingertips to the hollow between
tendons for some *Oh*. Then, *Sorry*. Glass shimmers

and swears a new life, constellation around the still-
echoing accident where it will get swept up and
discarded, into the gutter, perhaps, or a ditch along
the country road half-frozen over. Then a cloud

wraps itself over the moon in a *you-shouldn't-see-this*
draping, but it *should*, the moon should always see
the shards of glass in the neck to prevent conjuring
up a devil more merciful to stalk around the bed.

There will always be a worse apparition to sit
cross-legged, hard back to the headboard, putting
his hand in a silk pocket to add another icy stone,
to leave his breath of frost across the extra pillow.

And a body can be *turned on* like a machine,
but we don't say "I'm sorry, miss, but he's been
turned off." A body swears itself to another, swears
off another, coaxes *Just one more* in that little

bleating voice it feels cruel to refuse. Hex then haw, caesura between *Oh* and the *shit* that goes unsaid, leaving the *Oh* alone in bed, pissed off, making lists of all the wrongs in the world.

Confessional

Once my father lit our house on fire.
I drove my mother to the hospital,

kissed the shape of the doorknob
on her palm, and, when the burn changed

to bandage, killed the waiting room
lights. I saw what turns on after it's

turned off. All the old women's shrieks
were just birds trying out other tongues.

I loved to roll heroic names inside
my mouth in the new dark. Back home,

I made a nest of cigarette cartons and fake
opal jewelry sent from Hawaii after

the death of my Great Aunt. They hatched
barbed wire—I kept it to myself. I buried it

under the cherry blossom tree to guard
all my dead pets. This was before I held

the lighter to my skin in the co-ed bathroom,
before the drugs were no longer fun,

before my mother, the scientist, told me
how she used to pull the wings from

Japanese beetles to make them her own,
little buttons, dark thumbs she could

carry with her. When men tell me
what to call my body, I cannot help but think

transubstantiation. How what one shoves
under the microscope will be named harmful

or benign. Once, my father's death was
an excuse to stop eating. My mother's father

was an X-ray man, once a man of flash and bone.
Though I never met him, he tells me nightly

that a demon is an inverted god. Once,
there were two young pigeons in a cage,

whom I mistook for sparrows. Last night
a cricket jumped inside my mouth, replacing

the voice I spent so long trying to ignite.
Now all my heroes are beginning to revolt

me. I choke on every creation myth.
My name was never in any bible.

Homesteading with the Ghosts

You taught me how to truss a chicken with only the stem of a rose,
and when I bled you said I was paying respect to the animal.

What refused the dirt was suspicious—we were trying to live simple.
You learned to feel for the wishbone with your fingers and bury it

in the herb garden to dry out. Now, bones always smell like rosemary.
Once, in a fit, you threw all my books into the irrigation ditch,

where I found them later. It seems like this should have been beautiful,
some sort of gift. Like the whip you left under my pillow, dust-caked.

Winters are easier, as we soften. Bleeding out a bird onto the dirt
for dinner stains more than the thumbs. I study Gambel's quails while

you are sleeping, three in the morning, frost fingering the windows.
Polyandrous, females take multiple partners in a single breeding season.

They live in Mexico, which is the farthest away place I can imagine
when it's too cold to talk, and you are the only noise in the house.

Older females adopt the males' plumage and crow like them
underneath the mesquite, sound evaporating with the heavy wind.

Round Stories Arranged into a Square

We're in a round room. There are birds
bound to the wall. I mean dark shapes
the throat makes when opened toward
a scream. There is a purse strung
between two stars—no, a stomach.

—

We're in a round room. There are no
walls. Syringes hang from the necks
of leaves. No trees. Only drifted piles
we might have once known how to
occupy. We're in a round room,
dropped from some house we've never
entered. Undreamt, we are the only
touching branches. No skin. We have tools
for smoothing down surfaces. We have
tools for cutting down below the fat.
There is an animal asleep between us.

—

We're in a round room. There is a mattress
on the floor. Dark blue sheets. No,

a deep pool surrounded by a stone wall.
A well. Otters asleep between us, our
bodies the buoys keeping the bed afloat.

—

We're in a round room of glass.
A crowd gathers thick to observe us
stop dreaming each other up. There
is no other person who would understand
all this. The noise of water slapped
against window. How a body can get so
tangled in a wet, heavy sheet. We're in
a round room that revolves when
we close our eyes. We haven't learned
to open them. There is a fire escape.
Or there is a fire, but no stairs.
Or we never quite found legs
to climb them. Or there's no fire,
just a stairwell leading out, but we can't
see—into what? And so we stay put.

—

And Badly, Too

You do not want to be the girl who cries during hospital sitcoms, do not want to say yes please when what you mean is fuck off.

I want fireproof retinas, incombustible like my grandmother's safe, which someone tried to dynamite even though there wasn't anything valuable inside.

You do not want to be the bag of bones, the girl spray-painting *Brian Eno is God* on every stop sign. No silver huffing. Not the pretty ring around the mouth.

I do not want anything almond flavored. But I want to be bit numb, to be bit blue.

You mean you want to write an elegy for the cyber bully?

No, I want a cameo in a slasher film. Quiver and fletching, I want the arrow and the apple and the *stand there* trust.

Well, you want the hunting map, the hymnal, the white fur winter coat?

Quetzal, spoonbill, blue-footed booby—I want to catalogue all the wacko birds mother taught me.

You do or do not want a lozenge.

I want to lick someone's neck goodnight.

Yes, and yes you want the day to break into one large mirror-ball that metals its way into churches, saying silly things like *it will all be okay.*

I want to discover, finally, whether blue cherries and white raspberries exist.

You want to take a boy nap. To remember every lyric.

I want to remember—small song small song small song—the many silences I could dip my feet into.

So you want an alias.

I want a new towel, a scrap of faith, a clean tool.

Diurnal

I am done with you. I have said that. A person can
say things that cleave open the roof like a falling tree.
The body can be torn off without ever being touched.

A person can mistake herself for the bee that stings her.
The stinger can be dropped to the ground after it has been
worked out. The body can meet it there, cheek to

wood, when outside the clouds move so quickly
across the sky. A part of it has been torn off too—
the sky. All the bats toppled out of nightfall like it was

an accident. Nothing occurring to more than one creature
is ever an accident. The complicit nature of two.
We are making decisions together. She boils water

for her coffee, my tea. A person can sing in the shower
until her skin feels ready to peel off. She can sit
on the floor until she's convinced herself the ground

will open up for her in the midst of the next big
storm. I can't pull her up from there, or find
a clean towel to dry her hair. I am trying to decide

what to do with her, since a person can be done with.
I take pictures of myself in the mirror with my father's old
Polaroid. A body can be cut in two, so that an envelope

is full of only shoulders and necks. The girl on the floor
can be made to write *hospital* on two envelopes
with no return address. She doesn't cry from the sting,

though the welt is growing. At times, a body can
no longer see with the lights turned on. I mail
the envelope with my half-bodies and think about

who will open it. Someone can reconstruct our faces
in a brutal manner. Better than we ever could.
When the wind gets louder, I, too, sit down, facing

away from her. I try not to be selfish, always water
the plants at least once before they yellow, grow stiff.
Before all their leaves snap off, the veins become

a map for neglect. I undress slowly so I can see
where she is different from me. She has grown feathers
from her scalp. The howl of a distant wolf claws out

of her throat. But, beyond that, we have the same
birthmark on our nipples, same un-photogenic
mouths. A hole opens up like a tattoo in our chests.

To Have & To Hold

I back away from the fox with my nightmare hands. They are good at building only the make-believe. They spill water from any receptacle. They break a glass, which I step over later.

*

To avoid myself, I say every single thing that I really mean. I say *I can feel my body in time.* Or, *No, I can feel time inside my body.* Sometimes I have lost my body inside a forest I visited as a child. Something terrible must have happened there.

*

Nothing terrible ever happened there.

*

The hands between us confirm this. My hand is between nothing. It is the final wall in an empire with a ruined city on the other side.

*

There is a single burnt tree in a group of many. No one would catch her fire. No one burned with her.

*

I put my hand on the bark and pretend I am the arsonist. This makes me feel better. This makes me feel like I have done something important. Trees are not designed to inhabit our shortcomings.

*

I fall asleep on the pine-needled soil. The forest is bright with insect-sound. I wake to a mouth of teeth belonging to a creature that could probably never kill me.

*

A man is skinning the red fur in every dream I have. There is no blood, just the hair falling in pools. He does not do a good job, and when he is finished, he drapes his body over the fox's—flayed, new stench—and somehow he fits perfectly. Somehow they become one beast.

*

Once a swan bit my hand as I offered it a slice of white bread. Once my grandmother gave me a fur jacket I never tried on. Once I woke to a forest with the red light of morning pouring into my body, backlighting every bone through the thick skin of my palm.

Dirge: For Pompeii

Language become
combustible, lips gathering
themselves together,
the tongue's up-flip
toward its mouth's
ridged roof, each breath
whirring itself out
toward utterance's
smallest flame. A flame
we carried inside us,
spilling smoke down
the stairwell as if
we wanted someone—
but only if she hurried—
to follow us. Even
street signs gave away
their lettering to the fire
we once had a word for,
washing hands of
our indirection once
and for all. And who
could blame them?
Better to be a ghost
among the living if
the living can't
remember how to get
back to ghost. There were
places I went to when
the stars turned on,
places that put my body
together as if they knew
what I carried. I
found ashes hidden
within the creases
of our skin, but
we kept searching
each other, like lovers,
having forgotten
what it means to burn.
Direct my   your   ,
my   O

Covenant

The already dried-out fir you kicked down in early autumn, saying
it wasn't going to make it.

Which provided a manner of constellation for the journey—
grubs writhing at

the roots replaced the stars; we looked down for directions.
Fog came out

of the ground to remind us it, too, was alive, and thus had
its own nothing.

We readjusted our packs. We fled farther into the woods, became
attentive

to the crypt of blue, broken-open eggs inside a fallen nest,
the flickering

call of a coyote. I looked up, broke our agreement to stay true
to the ground.

Beyond a clearing, the streambed with the deer bloating inside it.
Skin loosening.

No blood. The space between its antlers formed an empty
bowl. Rope

of light thinning out between the tree trunks. I gathered
stones,

removed my sweatshirt to carry them. The water so
cold on my ankles

I almost growled. Water bugs fanned out from the deer
while I tied the shirt

around its neck. All this time you sat on your heels, were
watching me.

And I saw the uselessness, saw that my persistence created
a rift. The soil

I should have kept watching. And I tried to lift the body
up, but couldn't.

You didn't move to help. You were a stone or a bear or
were waiting

for the next tree to fell. You looked hungry. I used my foot
to shove it off

into the one deep pool. The deer sank, almost too quickly.
I wanted

to go back to the car for a flashlight. It was getting
dark

and the body had been too heavy—I was breathing hard,
not yet used to

being defeated. Your face turned away, too cold to touch.
I would not catch

a fish with my bare hands. Not that night. There would be
no fire. So, the car,

the flashlight I pretended to need. An exit point.
You said *I'll wait for you here.*

That was when I realized the possibility of never
coming back.

Against the Reification of Isadora Duncan

If you obscure nothing, there is no dark to remember.
—Francis Ponge

Where did you get your tragic expression?

Ophelia, Narcissus, blade of grass in my mouth, the dirt's
push & pulse, the way it moves through my hips

What is your music?

Things as they are crashing then burned

Gooseneck, red-ribboned you, what of apparitions?

Alone in the garden, I was passed right through. I was made a
caryatid. I was made a flue

And did you dance for her?

She placed a motor in my stomach. When she handed me the
sword and the cape, she also made me the bull

A muse?

She made me her salt lick. It was always about to rain when
she came

When you left for Europe on the cattle-boat, did you dance for the animals?

Their tongues held the beat of the ocean. Their hooves knew
no plan

Under starvation, did your feet turn cold?

Not as cold as the winter Seine

When your children went down in it?

When it swallowed them whole. When it spat up only a
tin cup. When it stopped reflecting the bridges, the
Belle Époque buildings, the barge

And the nurse?

And the nurse. And the children. And the car

What of fire and brimstone? What of grief?

I'll teach you how to hide it under a tunic, how to make the
windpipe a pulley, dredging up the ocean in your
chest. Never make it a concrete thing to form to a tune

Will you tie up your hair?

Not for all the butter in Paris. Not for the danse macabre in
my knees

Will you put on your shoes?

Not for stone. Not for glass. Not for you

Valediction Lessons

When I said forever I meant vector
from redwing to pullet. I meant quarantine

from a wonderfully complex disease.
When I said yes to the farm I meant fresh

eggs and a stranger's work. Every promise
a birdlife of receipts for pastry flour

and a house full of empty rooms. Face
to face, I think I loved you. What did you

expect? My hands can rest but they'd rather
be out in the middle of the river, entering

a swift current, alone with the trout. I think
I said this once. When I said it I meant

taxidermy may preserve the body, but it
can never keep the animal still long enough.

Bestiary

after Borges

Start with eggs. The violence of metal fork against window.
The omelet must be perfectly collapsing. In the state of. If a wasp

flies inside, take it to bed. There are worse things that could make
you love them. But the eggs. Apply yourself, like mother always

said: fly with your wings on straight. You may feel the drowned
animal that is always coming back to you. It cannot answer your

song every morning. The eggs fancy themselves hatching out
dragons. It's not so easy to admire the monster. The ancients

believed that any barking dog could unhinge itself toward
evil. Eggshell. Teeth. The blood inside the yolk. You have

grown awfully brave and alone while keening the generations
of minotaurs before you, haven't you. Have you lost all worship

for the present-day bestiary, the one that forms if you open your eyes
wide enough. Do you feel like you belong in celestial spaces.

You're searching for your keys while driving. You're scraping
the leftovers into the trash before you break open a single egg.

Aren't you always thinking you could have been the mammoth inside
the iceberg that didn't have a soul to tell her how beautiful her tusks.

Hermetic

> Demons bring adultery, murder, violence to one's father, sacrilege, ungodliness, strangling, suicide from a cliff and all such other demonic actions.
>
> —*The Way of Hermes*

A demon breathed into my dreaming mouth
(I promised I'd tell you everything)
a barnful of owls.

In their beaks black coils of telephone wires,
coils and coils,
and I could hear every last conversation on earth.

No one listened to each other, only talked
as if they were drowning
and had to buoy themselves up with words.

The owls did not look particularly disturbed,
or regal.
They were, perhaps, wicked,

as they mocked my own abeyance, cold-boned, featherless,
nothing remarkable
to hold under my tongue.

My 31 teeth (I said I would be truthful)
huddled in the wing-flung air, and the demon
hummed through the spaces

between each tooth, fermata
that turned my blood to marl.
There is the barn, and there is the gallery of bodies

buried beneath it. There is the gun rack I've never seen,
but know exists, because I built it last night.
I placed my underwear over it to dry,

and was proud of my craftiness.
I knelt in front of myself in the mirror
and was proud to believe in no other.

The demon asked me (don't turn away now)
what body part I'd give up
not to have let him have me. I told him

how soft the undersides of your wrists were.
I told him what I told you—I'll be steadfast
while sleeping. I'll sleep until I'm true.

Elegy

for David A. Van Landingham

Summer David. Coastal David. My David of the bag
of weed in the garage. The greasy hair, the Myer's &
OJ. David without a middle name, David of initials,
the *A.*, which, while on a small beach in Mexico—
mother joked—stood for *Arturo.* David of the rolling
r's, the hatred of California, David who stole his
mother's car and spent a night in jail. Photographer
of nude women not my mother. David of always
running out of gas. My David of the river, god of
oars, the raft its own country and I, princess of deer
and their diseases on the shore. Awestruck David.
Of always mispronouncing *Sartre.* Sci-fi David, man
with the smile like a slit in the tent. River otters
fed from his hand, David of water creatures. Who
showed me the recoiling of a sea anemone, slightest
prodding. David of failed kidneys. Of affliction,
midnight walker, gesturing out to the driveway,
the ditch trail, waterfall gravid with rain. Please.
The moss-covered rocks. David, the unsteady gait.

David. The hawk flying down to the wrist. Bones visible through skin, my David. Of translucence. David untouched. I still don't know what to do with his hands.

Other Techniques for Elegant Boatmanship

Triumph my poorly tied
knot, these inadequate

moorings and feel the choke
of sea air

somewhere near
the sternum. Brave Doctor,

Juan Gris never gave you
a body to break.

The suspension
of anchor in silt might be

vector, might be ache in crystal latticework,
but I'm no physicist.

Explain to me the body,
Doctor. Explain me away.

Excuse the machinery
of my ship—I'm feeling lazy.

Last night the dock-thief
combed my hair

with the legs
of ghost crabs,

but I didn't chastise his perpetuating
the ephemeral fetish.

His juke-joint mouth stole my writ
and the bone I keep

under my tongue
in case of hazard.

The body is not so dissimilar, dear,
to your ship—

but I've been rodeoing so long
I can't make a mouth of it.

I am *that* telescope owner
moonlighting as interested.

All my paper wasps
drowned in a tub of gasoline

and are now the floaters
haunting the corners of my eyes.

If you can't see,
I'll steer for you.

I'll cut your hair
over the edge so you can watch yourself

fall to pieces
in green water.

You can check my pulse
with a sand dollar's echo.

My reflexes with a bevy
of small, silver fish.

Here is my hull, Doctor,
my galley. And I'm starboard

and we're starflung, dumb bodies
emptied of need.

Hungry gulls
create our auguries.

Last Year at Marienbad

after Alain Resnais

Tell me how to make a bid against the probability of being frozen,

the way the sumac berries—*I was waiting for you*—
stayed so red in their clusters for a whole winter, and how love, too,
is that sleepy place of keeping still, or else

the one week of winter in summer, if we're to believe
what other people say.

Or else we say nothing at all,
watching the actress look away from the drawing of the garden.
She forgets Karlstadt, Marienbad, Baden-Salsa,
or has never visited the château's long corridors, forgets

the pitched seductions
amid statues, statues, fountains. All the ghosts of pearl,
their weather-talk. The lit chandeliers.

Rosencrantz (voice in the wilderness): . . . What's the game?
Guildenstern: What are the rules?

Misère—
the games that are played to lose.

Pretend the voiceovers aren't recounting every cabin we never
built. Or maybe we did. Maybe we spent a summer in some

pine-filled valley and made chairs with our hands.
It could be there still, beneath three feet of snow.

Consider all the rooms
that refuse us. The weather that outlasts us.

Yield Stress

Before skinned rabbits hung upside-down
from the dogwood. After I lied about

having ever killed a single thing. Before
I lied about whether or not I knew how

to handle a rifle. After all, all I have
are these hands. Only old women can

separate truth from bullet holes. Before
the pocketed knife became a family

secret. After secrets. After a continent
split in two under my grandmother's

feet. Before the field was razed, not
harvested. Before I was the field,

and allergic to myself. Or you. I am
always forgetting how you permeate

each landscape. After the dam went up
all I could think of was your hand

against my throat. Before my dress
snagged on the barbed wire fence.

Before the ring was purchased, then
pawned, there were mountains still

returning to their first selves after
years of glaciers pinned them back.

I mean held. Who is to say *true*
form. Here I am, a pilgrim atop frozen knees.

After a decade, here I have gone soft with
new heat. Here I am, thawing,

here is my sex-swollen tongue.
(It was yours it was yours it was yours)

When You Look Away, the World

Before I studied the whales my grandmother adopted for me, I found a half-jaw wedged in the dirt under her deck. I am almost always half-embarrassed. I take pictures of the day-moon, but it never shows up in my cell phone camera. I love the imprecise and jumpy squirrels. With a handful of sea glass I can predict the shape of not-here by putting the pieces together in my head. But Indiana's ocean carved itself back into the earth. Wind turbine—you're overdone. Ditto cornfield. Ditto stars. Please though, can I keep the stars? And conjugated verbs denoting habit. I love those. What they become predicts small futures. Somewhere, the season of dryness is welcomed. There is a room full of smuggled space rocks; it wouldn't help to call that my mind. Plankton does not love another plankton, but I don't live to be sifted through something larger than myself. Neither does the young man boasting of being the forty-second best pool player in a very small town. Nor anyone else on a sulfured spring morning. We were purists then, grandmother and I. We named a whale Nurse. We never spoke of the room where she kept her dinosaur skeleton, the one that sang out when we played games to improve our memory, having to remember which card had the cowboy hat. Which card had the spur.

What You Erase Knits Back Together

It's true, the lake at night does not want you.
        It is not inked up for a body—not yours.
There are rocks that have gone untouched

        for days; their needs are both nonexistent
and greater. A bottle should not remind you
        of yourself. Not tonight. Not when a bee

has drowned inside it. Do not think
        mausoleum. You are no Francis—birds
do not harken to your shoulders. Angels

        have swum right past the dock with no
particular sadness, but you weren't there
        to see them. There is something ordinary

about the wake they've left behind. It does not
        glow, not like the top-heavy willows now
semi-drowned. After light, the fish do not

        bother with bereavement, are not doubtful
nor devoted. The plunder inside a raccoon
        carcass is all grub and dark wing—both

twinning and emptying the body. What you see
        out here expands beneath the skin until a lung
is but a wallet, guffawing something silver into

        the air. Avoid the splinter that will still
work its way into your heel. When
        you call out in pain, make it a day-long

anthem, sent back into the footsteps
        you've been retracing since you left
the house with all those spiders.

        All those spiders curled together,
each dark leg touching each dark leg
        in small, white sacks beneath your bed.

Eclogue

Tonight, you are taping
X-rays to the lamp,

projecting your disease onto the living room
so that the bladder drapes
an accent wall.

Dark growth turns moss
touching down on top of the piano.

You mention the single deer
outside the window,
how winter's bluelight
fashions a basin from his sunken ribcage.

—

Photographer,
your slide show is not enough to interrupt the wildlife.
Put on your coat.
When the snow melts
you will be trackless and waning.

Even the early star
is only half-wild above the junipers
because wild is a process
that has to be learned.

To Have & To Hold

So I crush the pine needles, rubbing a cluster of them between my two palms until the scent is carried into my skin.

*

I normally watch the forest change around me like a stop-motion film. But really, it's just that I've kidnapped winter, shoved it down my throat for safekeeping, a key to some chastity belt.

*

Yes, I am standing here, harbinger of frost, waiting for a creature to look like it might have missed me. Like some coyote, some hare *wanted* my ice storm.

*

I will be here for years, this I have realized. I am being punished out in the open, which is why all the mice scatter away from my bare feet.

*

Auspice with the ammunition of omen, the way the ravens spread thin across a yellowing sky tells me, *Go home—you are a fool for light.* Me, explaining to each hole in the ground, *I won't hurt you.*

*

I know the lie. The brutal condition of having hands.

*

What stones can be raised up above a head, and how it only seems as if gravity is what brings their heaviness down. Some other surge, unspeakable.

*

Tomorrow under the rotted-out pine there will be a patch of snow. Beside it, one wing of a hawk left untouched by a fox's hot mouth.

*

I will have run a fever. I will have stunned the forest into submission, grown bored, and wandered unapologetically away into a new season, same hands.